FACT OR FICTION?

Eliot Ness

Tammy Gagne

Mitchell Lane
PUBLISHERS
P.O. Box 196
Hockessin, DE 19707
www.mitchelllane.com

Mitchell Lane
PUBLISHERS

Printing   1   2   3   4   5   6   7   8

Audie Murphy
Buffalo Bill Cody
The Buffalo Soldiers
Eliot Ness

Francis Marion
Robin Hood
The Tuskegee Airmen
Wyatt Earp

Library of Congress Cataloging-in-Publication Data
Gagne, Tammy.
 Eliot Ness / by Tammy Gagne.
     pages cm. — (Fact or fiction?)
 Includes bibliographical references and index.
 ISBN 978-1-61228-956-4 (library bound)
 1. Ness, Eliot—Juvenile literature. 2. United States. Federal Bureau of Investigation—Officials and employees—Biography—Juvenile literature. 3. Law enforcement—United States—Biography—Juvenile literature I. Title.
 HV7911.N45G34 2016
 363.2092—dc23
 [B]
                                                            2015010442

eBook ISBN: 978-1-61228-957-1

                                                            PBP

CONTENTS

Words in **bold** throughout can be found in the Glossary.

Eliot Ness made it his life's work to crack down on organized crime in Chicago. His biggest goal was to send gangster Al Capone to prison.

CHAPTER 1

Prohibition

In 1919 the United States ratified the Eighteenth Amendment to the Constitution and it went into effect the following year. The amendment made it illegal to produce, transport, and sell alcoholic beverages. Along with the Volstead Act—which gave "teeth" to the amendment by spelling out the methods by which it would be enforced—it ushered in what became known as the Prohibition era. Millions of Americans approved of the new measures. Millions more didn't. They wanted to keep consuming alcoholic beverages.

To satisfy this demand, gangsters saw Prohibition as a financial opportunity. They knew that many people would buy alcohol even though it was now illegal. And they also knew they could make a great deal of money selling it. This activity was commonly called **bootlegging**.

No one is more closely connected with Prohibition and bootlegging than Al Capone. Though he died in 1947, he remains one of the best-known criminals who ever lived.

Selling alcohol was just one of the many illegal ways Capone amassed immense sums of money. Born in 1899, he grew up in a rough part of Brooklyn in

Al Capone did not see himself as a criminal, but as a skilled businessman meeting the demands of the public.

New York City. By the time he was a teenager, he had been a member of two different gangs. Stealing, in one form or another, quickly became his career. But it was the Prohibition era that defined him. In 1920s Chicago, Capone became the symbol of the organized crime that controlled the city. As he noted, "This American system of ours, call it Americanism, call it capitalism, call it what you like, gives to each and every one of us a great opportunity if we can only seize it with both hands and make the most of it."[1] Capone didn't see himself as a criminal. Instead, he thought of himself as a businessman, giving people a product they wanted.

As Jonathan Eig, who wrote a biography of Capone called *Get Capone: The Secret Plot that Captured America's Most Wanted Gangster*, noted, "Prohibition completely changed the fabric of our country. You had these criminals who were base characters, horrible men, but they provided a service that even stand-up citizens were interested in. All the moral values got turned inside out, and that's what made Prohibition so fascinating."[2]

In 1933 the Twenty-first Amendment repealed Prohibition—the first and only time a constitutional amendment has been reversed. But the nearly fourteen years the law was in place provided plenty of time for Capone to become a larger-than-life figure. He always seemed to be several steps ahead of the law. It certainly helped that he had so many people working for him. His partners in crime even included police officers who were willing to take bribes to ignore his lawbreaking. Many people, both on and off Capone's payroll, feared him. For a while it seemed no one could stop him.

Eliot Ness would finally change that.

Ness was an agent with the Prohibition Bureau. His job was to hunt down criminals who were making a living by violating the Prohibition laws. Unlike many cops who secretly worked for Capone, Ness took his job seriously. Ness knew that catching Capone was the most important step in stopping the organized crime destroying Chicago. Even when it seemed like he would never nab Capone, Ness refused to give up the fight.

Eliot Ness's determination to capture Al Capone was a huge part of what made both men so famous. Countless newspaper and magazine articles, books, and movies have been written about the pair. Through the years the stories have taken on a life of their own. Many paint Ness as the ideal hero. Others depict him as flawed. But what is the truth?

Prohibition made liquor an illegal substance. When federal agents would find liquor in a person's possession, they would take it away at once.

CHAPTER 2

The Untouchables

Ness was a driven man. Born in 1902, he was only in his early twenties when he began his career as a Prohibition agent in 1927. His first job was just a temporary one. But he was determined to move up in the ranks.

Ness was hired by his brother-in-law, Alexander Jamie, a senior manager in the Chicago office of the Prohibition Bureau. No one can say whether Ness would have been able to land the position without this useful connection. But he definitely made good use of the opportunity.

Jamie became a personal role model for the young man. "Eliot had always wanted to follow in Jamie's footsteps," writes Douglas Perry, author of *Eliot Ness: The Rise and Fall of an American Hero*. "The forty-five-year-old assistant Prohibition **administrator**, a former FBI agent, had been something of a father figure to Eliot over the years. Eliot's actual father, Peter Ness, rarely took a day off from the thriving wholesale bakery business he owned, so it was the tall, grim-faced Jamie who had taught Eliot how to drive a car and shoot a gun. It was Jamie who had taught him about the importance of honesty in all things."[1]

Ness's first targets were bootleggers in Chicago Heights, an industrial city about 30 miles south of downtown Chicago. Prohibition had turned the Chicago Heights neighborhoods from peaceful communities into areas known for crime, including what the *Chicago Tribune* called "a great alcohol cooking ring."[2]

Numerous murders were taking place in Chicago Heights at this time. Several mob bosses wanted to be in charge. They would do anything to make that happen. They killed one another. They killed people they suspected of talking to the police. And, claims Perry, they even killed the city's chief of police, Lester Gilbert, when he made it clear that he wouldn't give in to bribes.

Jamie planned on taking down the Chicago Heights criminals, beginning with a bootlegger named Joe Martino. He would then try to scare the other bootleggers by making them think that Martino had linked them to various crimes. Ness played a key role in the success of the operation. But the two men soon realized that the Chicago Heights criminals answered to an even bigger mob boss: Al Capone.

In 1929, acting on a directive from President Herbert Hoover, federal agents began seeking methods of putting Capone behind bars. Some looked for evidence to accuse him of income tax evasion. Additionally, Ness was placed in charge of a special squad of Prohibition agents who wanted to hamper Capone's ability to make money by shutting down his illegal breweries and the warehouses where he stored liquor. Newspapers soon nicknamed the squad "The Untouchables" because none of them would take bribes. Their main weapon was a massive truck with a steel battering ram that would demolish building doors. The Untouchables would swarm inside and destroy the alcohol they found there.

Ness worked tirelessly. When he got married, he even refused to take a honeymoon trip with his new bride. "Eliot was too ambitious," Perry writes about this point in Ness's career. "He wanted to get ahead in the bureau, move up the ladder. In his five years with the Chicago office, he had never even considered taking a sick day. Now that he was leading his own unit, he worked even longer hours—through the night and every weekend. He stayed hyper-focused on the task at hand. Capone, always Capone."[3]

When Capone was finally arrested in 1931, it wasn't for his illegal activities. Instead, the US government charged him with tax fraud. The Internal Revenue Service (IRS) alleged that Capone owed $215,080.48 in unpaid income taxes.[4]

Chicago Tribune writer John Byrne explains why the government chose to focus on this aspect of his wrongdoing: "He was convicted for tax evasion, and not on any of the more than 5,000 counts in Ness' bootlegging indictment. [U.S. Attorney George E.Q.] Johnson reportedly feared that a jury might be too sympathetic to Capone's **moonshining** activities since Prohibition was so unpopular, but he figured jurors would convict a tax cheat."[5]

Actor Robert Stack played Eliot Ness in the popular ABC television series called **The Untouchables.**

Decline . . . and Rise

With Capone behind bars, Ness moved on to other assignments First he transferred to Cincinnati, then in 1935 to Cleveland, where he was soon appointed as public safety director and attracted praise for modernizing the city's police and fire departments. He was forced to resign seven years later after being involved in an automobile accident in which alcohol almost certainly was a factor. He ran for mayor of Cleveland in 1947 and was soundly defeated.

By then the famed Prohibition crusader had become a troubled alcoholic—a sad and ironic turn of events. He struggled to make ends meet with a succession of jobs. In all likelihood he would have sunk into obscurity, but in 1956 a friend introduced him to sportswriter and author Oscar Fraley. Fraley offered to help Ness write a **memoir**.

According to *Smithsonian* magazine, "Fraley embroidered Ness' recollections with accounts of gunplay and dime-novel tough talk and created a fiction with Ness as a solitary hero."[1] Ness apparently asked Fraley to change some of the more outrageous passages, but Ness died of a heart attack in May,

1957. The book, entitled *The Untouchables*, was published several months later. It remains unclear, therefore, how much of the book's content came from Ness himself and how much Fraley made up.

Jonathan Eig called the book "magical," but added that it is "mostly exaggerated, and maybe 10 percent of it is legitimate. The rest is baloney."[2]

However, *The Untouchables* was "prime rib" for Desi Arnaz. He and his wife, Lucille Ball (the star of the *I Love Lucy* television series of the 1950s), owned the Desilu television production company. Arnaz thought a series based on Ness's exploits would be successful. He was right. Starring Robert Stack as Ness, the series—also called *The Untouchables*—ran on the ABC network between 1959 and 1963. Eliot Ness became a household name for millions of Americans.

The story remained so popular that an 1987 movie version starring Kevin Costner did well at the box office and also received **critical** praise. Though nearly a century has passed since the Prohibition era began, Eliot Ness still remains a hero to many Americans.

"Eliot Ness is one of the most famous federal agents in the history of law enforcement," begins the web page of the U.S. government Bureau of Alcohol, Firearms, Tobacco and Explosives (ATF). "As a supervisor of an ordinary team of agents he did the extraordinary. Against all odds, he and his Untouchables broke the back of organized crime in Chicago, a city that was dubbed the 'Crime Capital of the World.' Ness performed brilliantly as both a crime fighter and a leader in a time of national

In 2014 United States Senators Dick Durbin and Mark Kirk proposed that the government rename the Bureau of Alcohol, Firearms, Tobacco and Explosives headquarters the Eliot Ness ATF Building.

distress."[3] In view of this high praise, it isn't surprising that early in 2014, US Senators Dick Durbin and Mark Kirk introduced legislation to rename the Bureau of Alcohol, Tobacco, Firearms and Explosives (BAFTE) headquarters in Washington, DC, after Eliot Ness.

Now
ON THE SCREEN!

DICK TRACY

WITH
Morgan CONWAY
Anne JEFFREYS
Mike...
...Jane GREER

K O
RADIO

Stories about Eliot Ness have taken on a life all their own over the years. Some people even say that Ness was the inspiration for crime-fighting comic book hero Dick Tracy.

CHAPTER 4

Clashing Viewpoints

Reaction to the proposal from the two senators came almost immediately from two Chicago aldermen who strongly opposed the idea. James Balcer and Ed Burke insisted that Ness was not the man most Americans think he was. "Eliot Ness never laid eyes on Al Capone," Burke stated. "The truth is—and we should tell the truth—Eliot Ness was a figment of Hollywood's imagination, and he had absolutely nothing to do with the case against Al Capone."[1]

Douglas Perry disagrees, at least in part: "We should indeed tell the truth, and the truth is that Burke is half right. He also completely misses the point. No, Ness didn't have anything to do with the income tax case against Capone. But Ness never claimed that he did. His job (and, yes, Ed, he did lay eyes on Capone) was to harass the Capone outfit and squeeze the mob boss's income stream. He and his 'Untouchables' team had significant success in this endeavor, risking their lives night after night. The team's wiretaps show that, just weeks after the Untouchables went into action, Capone's men had become **skittish**. After years of running the city, they no longer felt safe going about their business."[2]

Perry also notes, "In the summer of 1931, a week after Capone was **indicted** for income tax evasion, he also was indicted on Prohibition charges, with much of the evidence coming from Ness' squad."[3]

Today Eliot Ness is a bit of a mystery. What most people know about him are things they have learned from movies or television shows. These depictions contain a fair amount of **embellishment**. The story has been retold so many times that it seems less about history and more about entertainment value.

But it is clear from the ATF's website that he still commands great respect. It notes, "Perhaps what is most remarkable about Ness is not that he and his squad sent Capone packing for the **penitentiary**, but that he later went on to lead two additional teams of agents in the clean up of two equally crime-ridden cities protected by **corrupt** law enforcement agencies—Cincinnati and Cleveland."[4]

It adds that Ness was even the inspiration for the popular *Dick Tracy* comic strip. Its title character was a police detective as quick with his gun as he was clever. Cartoonist Chester Gould based his work on actual events involving Ness. "For decades thereafter," notes the ATF, "Eliot Ness and his fictional alter ego [Dick Tracy] would influence American notions of detective work, crime-fighting and heroism."[5]

Still another point of view comes from Jonathan Eig. His book paints a very different picture of Ness than *The Untouchables* did. "It's putting it generously to say Ness was the crime fighter who brought Capone to justice," he says. "Ness got the publicity, but not the end result. He may have harassed Capone in his bootlegging operation, but the final outcome had nothing to do with Ness."[6]

Even people outside the United States weigh in on the debate about Ness's hero status. British journalist David Leafe says, "Ness' courage and intelligence were beyond question. . . . When the Bureau set up a special squad to take on Capone . . . the quality which perhaps most recommended him for the job of leading it was his reputation for honesty . . . He was sickened by colleagues who took bribes."[7]

On the other hand, Leafe points out that Ness's high standards may have been exaggerated. "Legend has it that he scoured hundreds of personnel files, whittling them down until he was left with only the most outstanding agents in the bureau . . . In reality, he had to take whoever he could get since good men were hard to come by and regional bosses put up objections whenever Ness tried to [steal] theirs."[8]

Kevin Costner played Eliot Ness in **The Untouchables,** *the 1987 film about the federal agent's pursuit of Al Capone.*

Crossing the Line

While historians debate which accounts of Ness's life are true, other writers have turned Eliot Ness into a fictional character. One of them is William Bernhardt. His novel, *Nemesis: The Final Case of Eliot Ness*, follows Ness as he fights crime in Cleveland. The book's cover claims that it is "based on true events and new discoveries about Eliot Ness."[1]

Bernhardt mixes fact and fiction in the book, which centers on an actual unsolved case of a serial killer. He states, "I've always been fascinated by unsolved mysteries, cases that have captured the public imagination but have never been closed."[2] The book offers Bernhardt's imagined solution to the crimes.

Bernhardt's Ness shares the credit for the Al Capone case with the IRS. The title character admits, "People made fun of us for putting away a killer on such lame grounds. But it worked. Me and my boys kept him busy, preoccupied, a constant thorn in his side, while [IRS agent] Frank Wilson slowly put together a case proving Capone wasn't paying his taxes. We got him off the street, out of Chicago . . .

The tax charge did what we wanted. It put an end to the bloody reign of Al Capone."[3]

Like so many other writers, Bernhardt makes Ness out to be a hero. Both the character's actions and his **dialogue** are made up. But many of his words seem to be what the real Ness would have said. "In any city where corruption exists," he states in one fictional speech, "it follows that some officials are playing ball with the underworld. The dishonest public servant hiding behind a badge is more detestable than any street criminal or mob boss."[4]

We can find bits of truth about Eliot Ness in most of the stories told about him. But the majority of tales seem to move into the realm of fiction at one point or another. The television series, which starred Robert Stack as Ness, is an excellent example. "At first the show's producers drew heavily on events in the book. But after the series became a hit, they were forced to make things up,"[5] explains journalist Chris Larson.

Many events linked with Eliot Ness are the products of writers' imaginations. One of the best known is the scene from *The Untouchables* film in which a baby's life is endangered during a shootout between the Untouchables and Capone's men. "Scenes like the baby carriage rolling down the stairs at Union Station, or Ness tossing Capone henchman Frank 'the Enforcer' Nitti off a roof, never happened,"[6] adds Larson.

In 1958 Bob Fuesel began working for the IRS, where he met many former members of The Untouchables. Fuesel learned a great deal about the

Al Capone's conviction for income tax evasion wasn't the first time he was put behind bars. He was arrested in 1929 for carrying a concealed weapon. He spent eight months in luxury in this cell at Eastern State Penitentiary in Pennsylvania.

actual Capone case. He says, "It was during that time I came to understand the real Eliot Ness, and found out that Eliot Ness really didn't do anything (people said) he did, according to their testimony to me."[7] The impression Fuesel got from his IRS coworkers was that Ness barely left the office.

When *The Untouchables* movie was being filmed, Fuesel spoke with the film's star. "I told Kevin Costner, who I met with numerous times, that Eliot Ness really didn't do any of this, that basically he was afraid of guns. And he said to me 'Bob, Bob, Bob, this is Hollywood, we really don't [care]. We make it up as we go along,'"[8] Fuesel recalls. If his information about Ness is accurate, the movie was indeed misleading. Costner's character carries guns throughout the film. He reaches for them repeatedly, starting within the first fifteen minutes of the film.

The real Eliot Ness died in 1957, just ten years after his nemesis, Al Capone.

The Untouchables movie ends with Ness playing a major role in getting Capone on tax evasion charges. But even Ness's biggest supporters will admit that this is one of the many ways that Hollywood has adapted the story to make it more entertaining.

It is unlikely that the real Eliot Ness did all of the things his movie character does. But how do know which things are true and which ones aren't?

Douglas Perry holds writers accountable for many false impressions of Ness. "Alderman Burke is correct that Ness became a figment of Hollywood's imagination," Perry says. "Ness would not have recognized himself in either Robert Stack's or Kevin Costner's portrayal of him. But remember, in Hollywood, nobody knows anything. Chicago's City Council shouldn't hold that against Eliot Ness."[9]

The image we have created for Eliot Ness seems as powerful as his accomplishments, whether they were real or not. "Imagine if such a leader emerged in modern society with the skills to restore . . . the concept of faith and trust in the government?" asks the ATF. "Ness' contribution to the science of policing, along with his tireless pursuit of his vision of a professional police force, today, continues to serve as the standard of excellence in law enforcement leadership today."[10]

FACT OR FICTION?

Eliot Ness will forever be linked to mob boss Al Capone. Neither man's life story would be complete without the mention of the other one. Over time tales of the relentless federal agent and Chicago's most famous mob boss have come to include some questionable details. Both men have become larger-than-life characters. Surely, the stories are even more exciting with the thrilling twists and turns that Hollywood has added to them. But two very real men inspired these tales that have become such a complicated mix of fact and fiction.

The most basic truth about Ness is that he was not the brilliant mastermind who decided to charge Al Capone and his partners in crime with tax evasion. It was actually Internal Revenue Service agents who came up with this clever plan. But it is essential to remember that Ness himself never claimed this particular victory. It was moviemakers who credited him with the idea. And audience members ate up the embellishment. We mustn't think Ness a liar for a deception in which he played no part.

Eliot Ness was a dedicated government agent who wanted more than anything to send Al Capone to prison. Did he want to accomplish this goal for the fame that would come with it or the simple satisfaction of an incredible job well done? It is unlikely that we will ever know for sure. That answer went to the grave with Ness himself. Even his own memoir was finished by someone else.

Ness may not have been the gun-wielding hero that many of us have seen on film. But he is nonetheless still a significant historical figure. Many people even consider Eliot Ness a national hero. When he and his Untouchables were on the case, Capone and his men were clearly wary of being caught. Knowing that they were being watched, they had to work harder to conceal their illegal activity.

Is it important that in the end Ness was not the one to take down Capone? The answer to this question depends on whom you ask. Ness will always have a fair number of **critics**. Still, his supporters argue that his investigation and pursuit of Capone laid the groundwork for Capone's capture. But whether he earned every bit of his hero's status or not, the fact remains that he has become a symbol of honesty and integrity in the United States government's battle against organized crime. Eliot Ness was undoubtedly one of the good guys.

Chapter 1: Prohibition

1. Katherine Long, "Prohibition, Profits, and Power: Rise of the Gangster Entrepreneur." https://medium.com/audaces-fortuna-iuvat/prohibition-profits-and-power-rise-of-the-gangster-entrepreneur-4ede539b666d
2. Katherine Don, "How Real is 'Boardwalk Empire's' Al Capone?" *Salon*, October 11, 2010. http://www.salon.com/2010/10/11/boardwalk_empire_al_capone/

Chapter 2: The Untouchables

1. Perry, Douglas. *Eliot Ness: The Rise and Fall of an American Hero* (New York: Viking, 2014), p. 17.
2. Ibid., p. 26.
3. Ibid., p. 83.
4. Chicago Historical Society, Al Capone. http://www.chicagohs.org/history/capone/cpn3a.html
5. John Byrne, "Chicago aldermen: Eliot Ness overhyped." *Chicago Tribune*, February 28, 2014. http://articles.chicagotribune.com/2014-02-28/news/chi-chicago-aldermen-eliot-ness-overhyped-20140228_1_eliot-ness-the-untouchables-atf-hq

Chapter 3: Decline . . . and Rise

1. Erick Trickey, "Eliot Ness vs. J. Edgar Hoover." *Smithsonian*, October 2014, p. 107.
2. Michael Sneed, "Sneed exclusive: 'Get Capone' author says naming building for Eliot Ness 'a lousy idea.'" *Chicago Sun-Times*, January 13, 2014. http://www.suntimes.com/news/sneed/24940777-452/sneed-exclusive-get-capone-author-says-naming-building-for-eliot-ness-a-lousy-idea.html
3. Bureau of Alcohol, Tobacco, Firearms and Explosives, Eliot Ness. http://www.atf.gov/content/about/our-history/eliot-ness

Chapter 4: Clashing Viewpoints

1. Douglas Perry, "The truth about Eliot Ness." *Chicago Tribune*, January 24, 2014. http://articles.chicagotribune.com/2014-01-24/opinion/ct-eliot-ness-capone-atf-building-ed-burke-perspec-20140124_1_george-e-q-eliot-ness-capone-outfit
2. Ibid.
3. Ibid.

4. Bureau of Alcohol, Tobacco, Firearms and Explosives, Eliot Ness. http://www.atf.gov/content/about/our-history/eliot-ness
5. Ibid.
6. Michael Sneed, "Sneed exclusive: 'Get Capone' author says naming building for Eliot Ness 'a lousy idea.'" *Chicago Sun-Times*, January 13, 2014. http://www.suntimes.com/news/sneed/24940777-452/sneed-exclusive-get-capone-author-says-naming-building-for-eliot-ness-a-lousy-idea.html
7. David Leafe, "Womaniser. Drunk. The Untouchable cop who battled Al Capone and was no Hollywood hero." *Daily Mail*, March 7, 2014. http://www.dailymail.co.uk/news/articlc-2576061/Womaniser-Drunk-The-Untouchable-cop-battled-Al-Capone-no-Hollywood-hero.html
8. Ibid.

Chapter 5: Crossing the Line
1. William Bernhardt, *Nemesis: The Final Case of Eliot Ness* (New York: Ballantine Books, 2009), cover copy.
2. William Bernhardt, author website. http://www.williambernhardt.com/books/nemesis.php
3. William Bernhardt, *Nemesis*, p. 5.
4. Ibid., p. 121.
5. Chris Larson, "In print: Who was Eliot Ness?" *Chicago Reader*, February 11, 1999. http://www.chicagoreader.com/chicago/in-print-who-was-eliot-ness/Content?oid=898420
6. Ibid.
7. John Byrne, "Chicago aldermen: Eliot Ness overhyped." *Chicago Tribune*, February 28, 2014. http://articles.chicagotribune.com/2014-02-28/news/chi-chicago-aldermen-eliot-ness-overhyped-20140228_1_eliot-ness-the-untouchables-atf-hq
8. Ibid.
9. Douglas Perry, "The truth about Eliot Ness." *Chicago Tribune*, January 24, 2014. http://articles.chicagotribune.com/2014-01-24/opinion/ct-eliot-ness-capone-atf-building-ed-burke-perspec-20140124_1_george-e-q-eliot-ness-capone-outfit
10. Bureau of Alcohol, Tobacco, Firearms and Explosives, Eliot Ness. http://www.atf.gov/content/about/our-history/eliot-ness

administrator (ad-MIN-uh-stray-tuhr)—a person who manages affairs, especially business, school, or government

bootleg (BOOT-leg)—to produce or sell alcohol illegally

critic (KRIT-ik)—a person who makes or gives a judgment of the value, worth, beauty, or excellence of something

corrupt (kuh-RUHPT)—characterized by improper conduct

dialogue (DIE-uh-lawg)—conversation in a written story or play

embellishments (ehm-BELL-ish-muhnts)—fictitious additions to a narrative to make it more dramatic

indict (in-DITE)—to charge with an offense or crime

memoir (MEM-wahr)—a story of a personal experience

moonshining (MOON-shine-ing)—illegally producing whiskey from corn

penitentiary (pen-uh-TEN-shuh-ree)—a state or federal prison

skittish (SKIT-ish)—easily frightened

WORKS CONSULTED

Bernhardt, William. *Nemesis: The Final Case of Eliot Ness*. New York: Ballantine Books, 2009.

Bernhardt, William. Author website. http://www.williambernhardt.com/books/nemesis.php

Bureau of Alcohol, Tobacco, Firearms, and Explosives, Eliot Ness. http://www.atf.gov/content/about/our-history/eliot-ness

Byrne, John. "Chicago aldermen: Eliot Ness overhyped." *Chicago Tribune*, February 28, 2014. http://articles.chicagotribune.com/2014-02-28/news/chi-chicago-aldermen-eliot-ness-ovehyped-20140228_1_eliot-ness-the-untouchables-atf-hq

Chicago Historical Society, Al Capone. http://www.chicagohs.org/history/capone/cpn3a.html

Don, Katherine. "How Real is 'Boardwalk Empire's' Al Capone?" *Salon*, October 11, 2010. http://www.salon.com/2010/10/11/boardwalk_empire_al_capone/

Eig, Jonathan. "Actually, Eliot Ness Was Just a Nuisance to Al Capone." *Wall Street Journal*, January 16, 2014. http://online.wsj.com/news/articles/SB10001424052702304549504579320883052198424

History.com, The 18th and 21st Amendments. http://www.history.com/topics/18th-and-21st-amendments

Larson, Chris. "In print: Who was Eliot Ness?" *Chicago Reader*, February 11, 1999. http://www.chicagoreader.com/chicago/in-print-who-was-eliot-ness/Content?oid=898420

Leafe, David. "Womaniser. Drunk. The Untouchable cop who battled Al Capone and was no Hollywood hero." *Daily Mail*, March 7, 2014. http://www.dailymail.co.uk/news/article-2576061/Womaniser-Drunk-The-Untouchable-cop-battled-Al-Capone-no-Hollywood-hero.html

Long, Katherine. "Prohibition, Profits, and Power: Rise of the Gangster Entrepreneur." https://medium.com/audaces-fortuna-iuvat/prohibition-profits-and-power-rise-of-the-gangster-entrepreneur-4ede539b666d

Perry, Douglas. *Eliot Ness: The Rise and Fall of an American Hero*. New York: Viking, 2014.

Sneed, Michael. "Sneed exclusive: 'Get Capone' author says naming building for Eliot Ncss 'a lousy idea.'" *Chicago Sun-Times*, January 13, 2014. http://www.suntimes.com/news/sneed/24940777-452/sneed-exclusive-get-capone-author-says-naming-building-for-eliot-ness-a-lousy-idea.html

Trickey, Erick. "Eliot Ness vs. J. Edgar Hoover." *Smithsonian*, October, 2014.

The Untouchables (film). Paramount Pictures, 1987.

FURTHER READING

Blumenthal, Karen. *Bootleg: Murder, Moonshine, and the Lawless Years of Prohibition*. New York: Square Fish, 2013.

Gitlin, Martin. *The Prohibition Era*. Edina, MN: ABDO Publishing, 2011.

Lusted, Marcia Amidon. *The Roaring Twenties: Discover the Era of Prohibition, Flappers, and Jazz*. White River Junction, VT: Nomad Prcss, 2014.

Schwartz, Heather. *Gangsters, Bootleggers, and Bandits* (Shockzone: Villains). Minneapolis, MN: Lerner, 2013.

Yancey, Diane. *Heroes and Villains: Al Capone*. San Diego, CA: Lucent Books, 2002.

ON THE INTERNET

ATF for Kids, Eliot Ness
http://www.atf.gov/kids/about/eliot-ness/

Cleveland Police Museum, Eliot Ness
http://www.clevelandpolicemuseum.org/collections/eliotness.html

History Channel, Al Capone
http://www.history.com/topics/al-capone

ABOUT THE AUTHOR

Tammy Gagne is the author of numerous books for adults and children, including *Robin Hood* and *Tuskegee Airmen* for Mitchell Lane Publishers. She resides in northern New England with her husband and son. One of her favorite pastimes is visiting schools to speak to kids about the writing process.